Who's There?

501 Side-Splitting Knock-Knock Jokes from Highlights

Illustrated by Kelly Kennedy

Highlights Press
Honesdale, Pennsylvania

Highlights for Children, Inc.
P.O. Box 18201
Columbus Ohio 43218-0201
Printed in the United States of America
ISBN: 978-1-59078-918-6 (PB)

First edition

Visit our website at highlights.com.
10 9 8 7 6

Design by Barbara Grzeslo
Production by Margaret Mosomillo
The titles are set in Aachen.
The text is set in Bones.

CONTENTS

A Taste of Funny

Food Fit for Laughs

Knock, knock.
Who's there?
Pickle.
Pickle who?
Pickle little flower to give to your mother.

Knock, knock.
Who's there?
Banana.
Banana who?

Knock, knock.
Who's there?
Banana.
Banana who?

Knock, knock.
Who's there?
Orange.
Orange who?
Orange you glad I didn't say banana?

Knock, knock.
Who's there?
Salome.
Salome who?
Salome and cheese.

Knock, knock.
Who's there?
Cook.
Cook who?
Hey, who are you
     calling a cuckoo?

Knock, knock.
Who's there?
Cantaloupe.
Cantaloupe who?
We cantaloupe tonight—I forgot the
  ladder.

Knock, knock.
Who's there?
Apple.
Apple who?
Apple on the door
  but it doesn't open.

Knock, knock.
Who's there?
Kiwi.
Kiwi who?
Kiwi go to the store?

Knock, knock.
Who's there?
Pudding.
Pudding who?
Pudding on your shoes before your
   pants is a bad idea.

Knock, knock.
Who's there?
Figs.
Figs who?
Figs me a sandwich, please.

Knock, knock.
Who's there?
Turnip.
Turnip who?
Turnip the heat—it's cold in here.

Knock, knock.
Who's there?
Stew.
Stew who?
Stew early to go to bed.

Knock, knock.
Who's there?
Grub.
Grub who?
Grub hold of my hand and let's get out
    of here.

Knock, knock.
Who's there?
Carrot.
Carrot who?
Don't you carrot all about me?

Knock, knock.
Who's there?
Cheese.
Cheese who?
Cheese a very smart girl.

Knock, knock.
Who's there?
Mint.
Mint who?
I mint to tell you sooner.

Knock, knock.
Who's there?
Broccoli.
Broccoli who?
Broccoli doesn't have a last name, silly.

Knock, knock.
Who's there?
Water.
Water who?
Water you waiting for? Let me in.

Knock, knock.
Who's there?
Bacon.
Bacon who?
I'm bacon a cake for your birthday.

Knock, knock.
Who's there?
Candy.
Candy who?
Candy cow jump
over de moon?

Knock, knock.
Who's there?
Beets.
Beets who?
Beets me.

Knock, knock.
Who's there?
Wanda.
Wanda who?
Wanda have another hamburger?

Knock, knock.
Who's there?
Sauce.
Sauce who?
He sauce together yesterday.

Knock, knock.
Who's there?
Distressing.
Distressing who?
Distressing has too much vinegar.

Knock, knock.
Who's there?
Bean.
Bean who?
Bean fishing lately?

Knock, knock.
Who's there?
Truffle.
Truffle who?
What's the truffle with you?

Knock, knock.
Who's there?
Cereal.
Cereal who?
Cereal pleasure to meet you.

Knock, knock.
Who's there?
Pasta.
Pasta who?
Pasta salt and pepper, please.

Knock, knock.
Who's there?
Gravy.
Gravy who?
Gravy Crockett.

Knock, knock.
Who's there?
Dill.
Dill who?
Good-bye dill we meet again.

Knock, knock.
Who's there?
Pepper.
Pepper who?
A glass of juice will pepper up.

Knock, knock.
Who's there?
Pecan.
Pecan who?
Pecan somebody your own size.

Knock, knock.
Who's there?
Tuna.
Tuna who?
Tuna piano and it'll sound better.

Knock, knock.
Who's there?
Toast.
Toast who?
Toast were the days.

Knock, knock.
Who's there?
Chicken.
Chicken who?
Better chicken
    the oven—something's burning.

Knock, knock.
Who's there?
Cash.
Cash who?
No thanks, but I'd love some peanuts.

Knock, knock.
Who's there?
Irish stew.
Irish stew who?
Irish stew in the name of the law.

Knock, knock.
Who's there?
Butternut.
Butternut who?
Butternut come in—the floor's wet.

Knock, knock.
Who's there?
Butter.
Butter who?
Butter bring an umbrella—it looks like rain.

Knock, knock.
Who's there?
Raisin.
Raisin who?
We're raisin our hands before we speak.

Knock, knock.
Who's there?
Falafel.
Falafel who?
I falafel my bike and hurt my knee.

Knock, knock.
Who's there?
Haddock.
Haddock who?
I need an aspirin for my haddock.

Knock, knock.
Who's there?
Kansas.
Kansas who?
Kansas what soda comes in.

Knock, knock.
Who's there?
Pizza.
Pizza who?
Pizza taffy would taste good.

Knock, knock.
Who's there?
Ketchup.
Ketchup who?
Ketchup with me and
    I'll tell you.

Knock, knock.
Who's there?
Rice.
Rice who?
Rice up early every morning.

Knock, knock.
Who's there?
Omelet.
Omelet who?
Omelet smarter than you think.

Knock, knock.
Who's there?
Artichokes.
Artichokes who?
Artichokes when he gobbles his food.

Knock, knock.
Who's there?
Frankfurter.
Frankfurter who?
Frankfurter lovely present.

Knock, knock.
Who's there?
Celery.
Celery who?
Celery dance?

Knock, knock.
Who's there?
Ham.
Ham who?
Ham I getting warmer?

Knock, knock.
Who's there?
Guava.
Guava who?
Guava good time.

Knock, knock.
Who's there?
Wafer.
Wafer who?
Wafer the bus at the corner.

Knock, knock.
Who's there?
Mac.
Mac who?
Mac and cheese.

Knock, knock.
Who's there?
Handsome.
Handsome who?
Handsome of those cookies over, please.
I'm hungry.

Knock, knock.
Who's there?
Cumin.
Cumin who?
Cumin side—it's freezing out there.

Knock, knock.
Who's there?
Doughnut.
Doughnut who?
Doughnut open this
  until your birthday.

Knock, knock.
Who's there?
Almond.
Almond who?
Not almond like watching football.

Knock, knock.
Who's there?
Hummus.
Hummus who?
Hummus be kidding!

Knock, knock.
Who's there?
Annapolis.
Annapolis who?
Annapolis a day is good for you.

Knock, knock.
Who's there?
Hominy.
Hominy who?
Hominy times must I tell you?

Knock, knock.
Who's there?
Muffin.
Muffin who?
There's muffin the matter
    with me—I'm doing fine!

Knock, knock.
Who's there?
Lima bean.
Lima bean who?
Lima bean waiting for you to come over.

Knock, knock.
Who's there?
Curry.
Curry who?
Curry the groceries in, please.

Knock, knock.
Who's there?
Fajita.
Fajita who?
Fajita another thing, I'll be stuffed.

Knock, knock.
Who's there?
Honeycomb.
Honeycomb who?
Honeycomb your hair—it's tangled.

Knock, knock.
Who's there?
Honeydew.
Honeydew who?
Honeydew you love me?

Knock, knock.
Who's there?
Avocado.
Avocado who?
Avocado an awful cold.

Knock, knock.
Who's there?
Goudas.
Goudas who?
She's as goudas can be.

Knock, knock.
Who's there?
Ice cream.
Ice cream who?
Ice cream when
    I'm scared—don't you?

Howls About That?

All Things Hairy and Scary

Knock, knock.
Who's there?
Zombies.
Zombies who?
Only zombies in
   a hive make honey.

Knock, knock.
Who's there?
Witches.
Witches who?
Witches the way
    to go home?

Knock, knock.
Who's there?
Weirdo.
Weirdo who?
Weirdo you think you're going?

Knock, knock.
Who's there?
Fangs.
Fangs who?
Fangs for letting me in.

Knock, knock.
Who's there?
Voodoo.
Voodoo who?
Voodoo you think you are?

Knock, knock.
Who's there?
Howl.
Howl who?
Howl you know unless you open the
    door?

Knock, knock.
Who's there?
Spell.
Spell who?
W-H-O.

Knock, knock.
Who's there?
Crypt.
Crypt who?
She crypt up behind me.

Knock, knock.
Who's there?
Ogre.
Ogre who?
Please do it ogre again.

Knock, knock.
Who's there?
Gargoyle.
Gargoyle who?
If you gargoyle with salt water, your throat will
feel better.

Knock, knock.
Who's there?
Goblin.
Goblin who?
Goblin your food will give you a
tummyache.

Knock, knock.
Who's there?
Disguise.
Disguise who?
Disguise de limit.

Knock, knock.
Who's there?
Thumping.
Thumping who?
Thumping green and thlimy is crawling
    up your leg.

Knock, knock.
Who's there?
Twig.
Twig who?
Twig or tweat.

Knock, knock.
Who's there?
Boo.
Boo who?
Don't be scared—it's only a joke.

Knock, knock.
Who's there?
Vampire.
Vampire who?
The Vampire State Building.

Fins, Feathers, and Fur

Animal Antics

Knock, knock.
Who's there?
Llama.
Llama who?
"Llama Yankee
    Doodle Dandy . . ."

Knock, knock.
Who's there?
Walrus.
Walrus who?
Why do you walrus ask
that silly question?

Knock, knock.
Who's there?
Cock-a-doodle.
Cock-a-doodle who?
Not cock-a-doodle who, you silly chicken,
cock-a-doodle-doo!

Knock, knock.
Who's there?
Porpoise.
Porpoise who?
I stopped by on porpoise to see you.

Knock, knock.
Who's there?
Beagle.
Beagle who?
Beagle with cream cheese.

Knock, knock.
Who's there?
Lion.
Lion who?
You're lion down on the job again.

Knock, knock.
Who's there?
Ocelot.
Ocelot who?
You ocelot of questions, don't you?

Knock, knock.
Who's there?
Dragon.
Dragon who?
You're dragon your feet again.

Knock, knock.
Who's there?
Stork.
Stork who?
Better stork up on food before the
    storm.

Knock, knock.
Who's there?
Feline.
Feline who?
I'm feline fine, thanks.

Knock, knock.
Who's there?
Baby owl.
Baby owl who?
Baby owl see you later or
baby owl just call you.

Knock, knock.
Who's there?
Cows.
Cows who?
Cows say "moo," not "who."

Knock, knock.
Who's there?
Pooch.
Pooch who?
Pooch your coat on—it's cold outside.

Knock, knock.
Who's there?
Viper.
Viper who?
Please viper runny nose.

Knock, knock.
Who's there?
Wren.
Wren who?
Wren you're finished, please put it away.

Knock, knock.
Who's there?
Gorilla.
Gorilla who?
Gorilla cheese sandwich for me, will you,
    please?

Knock, knock.
Who's there?
Rhino.
Rhino who?
Rhino every knock-knock joke there is.

Knock, knock.
Who's there?
Beaver E.
Beaver E who?
Beaver E quiet and nobody will hear us.

Knock, knock.
Who's there?
Weevil.
Weevil who?
Weevil stay only a few minutes.

Knock, knock.
Who's there?
Ostrich.
Ostrich who?
Ostrich my arms up to the sky.

Knock, knock.
Who's there?
Mammoth.
Mammoth who?
Mammoth is sthuck 'cause I'th been
   eatin' peanut buther.

Knock, knock.
Who's there?
Grrr.
Grrr who?
Are you a bear or an owl?

Knock, knock.
Who's there?
Moose.
Moose who?
Moose you be so nosy?

Knock, knock.
Who's there?
Goat.
Goat who?
Goat to the door and find out.

Knock, knock.
Who's there?
Aardvark.
Aardvark who?
Aardvark a hundred miles for you.

Knock, knock.
Who's there?
Kanga.
Kanga who?
Kangaroo, silly.

Knock, knock.
Who's there?
Spider.
Spider who?
In spider everything, I still like you.

Knock, knock.
Who's there?
Alpaca.
Alpaca who?
Alpaca the trunk, you pack-a the
  suitcase.

Knock, knock.
Who's there?
Iguana.
Iguana who?
Iguana hold your hand.

Knock, knock.
Who's there?
Bat.
Bat who?
I'll bat you can't guess.

Knock, knock.
Who's there?
Amoeba.
Amoeba who?
Amoeba right, but I could be wrong.

Knock, knock.
Who's there?
Gnats.
Gnats who?
Gnats not a bit funny.

Knock, knock.
Who's there?
Panther.
Panther who?
Panther what I wear on my legth.

Knock, knock.
Who's there?
Weasel.
Weasel who?
Weasel while you work.

Knock, knock.
Who's there?
Worm.
Worm who?
It's worm in here, isn't it?

Knock, knock.
Who's there?
Flea.
Flea who?
Flea blind mice.

Knock, knock.
Who's there?
Roach.
Roach who?
I roach you a letter—did you get it?

Knock, knock.

Who's there?

Aware.

Aware who?

"Aware, aware has my little dog gone?"

Knock, knock.

Who's there?

Pig.

Pig who?

Pig up your feet or you'll trip.

Knock, knock.
Who's there?
Halibut.
Halibut who?
Halibut we go to the movies tonight?

Knock, knock.
Who's there?
Urchin.
Urchin who?
Urchin has a dimple.

Knock, knock.
Who's there?
Termites.
Termites who?
Termite's the night we're going out.

Knock, knock.
Who's there?
Mice.
Mice who?
Mice to meet you.

Knock, knock.
Who's there?
Me.
Me who?
You sure have a funny-sounding cat.

Knock, knock.
Who's there?
Toucan.
Toucan who?
Toucan play this game.

Knock, knock.
Who's there?
Owls.
Owls who?
Of course they do—
      everybody knows that.

Knock, knock.
Who's there?
Detail.
Detail who?
Detail of de cat is on de end.

Knock, knock.
Who's there?
Rabbit.
Rabbit who?
Please rabbit up for me—it's a present for
    my mom.

Knock, knock.
Who's there?
Toad.
Toad who?
Toad you I knew all the knock-knock jokes.

Knock, knock.
Who's there?
Heifer.
Heifer who?
Heifer dollar is better than none.

Knock, knock.
Who's there?
Alli.
Alli who?
Alligator, that's who.

Knock, knock.
Who's there?
Bug spray.
Bug spray who?
Bug spray that snakes and birds will stay away.

The Daily Grin(d)

Jokes on the Job

Knock, knock.
Who's there?
Farmer.
Farmer who?
I hope I get a dog farmer birthday.

Knock, knock.
Who's there?
Butcher.
Butcher who?
"You butcher left leg in,
   you butcher left leg out . . ."

Knock, knock.
Who's there?
Little old lady.
Little old lady who?
Wow—I didn't know you could yodel!

Knock, knock.
Who's there?
Police.
Police who?
Police stop telling knock-knock jokes.

Knock, knock.
Who's there?
Unite.
Unite who?
When unite Lancelot, he joins the
    Round Table.

Knock, knock.
Who's there?
Major.
Major who?
Major open the door, didn't I?

Knock, knock.
Who's there?
A little boy.
A little boy who?
A little boy who can't reach the doorbell.

Knock, knock.
Who's there?
Stepfather.
Stepfather who?
One stepfather and you'll be inside.

Knock, knock.
Who's there?
Teachers.
Teachers who?
Teachers for the red, white, and blue.

Knock, knock.
Who's there?
Jester.
Jester who?
Jester minute—
   I'm trying to find my keys.

Knock, knock.
Who's there?
Warrior.
Warrior who?
Warrior been all my life?

Knock, knock.
Who's there?
Waiter.
Waiter who?
Waiter minute while I tie my shoes.

Knock, knock.
Who's there?
Queen.
Queen who?
Queen as a whistle.

This and That

Take Your Pick

Knock, knock.
Who's there?
Clothesline.
Clothesline who?
Clothesline all over the floor end up
    wrinkled.

Knock, knock.
Who's there?
Avenue.
Avenue who?
Avenue heard the good news?

Knock, knock.
Who's there?
Cargo.
Cargo who?
Cargo beep, beep.

Knock, knock.
Who's there?
Bed.
Bed who?
Bed you can't guess who I am.

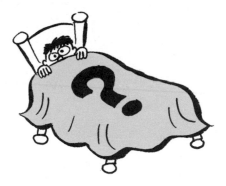

Knock, knock.
Who's there?
Uphill.
Uphill who?
Uphill will help your headache go away.

Knock, knock.
Who's there?
Maple.
Maple who?
I maple the door off its hinges if you don't
  open it.

Knock, knock.
Who's there?
White.
White who?
I'm white in the middle of something.

Knock, knock.
Who's there?
I'm.
I'm who?
Don't you know who you are?

Knock, knock.
Who's there?
Bayou.
Bayou who?
I'll bayou a treat.

Knock, knock.
Who's there?
Spin.
Spin who?
Spin too long since we saw each other.

Knock, knock.
Who's there?
Atomic.
Atomic who?
I have atomic ache.

Knock, knock.
Who's there?
Tree.
Tree who?
Tree more days till vacation.

Knock, knock.
Who's there?
Thermos.
Thermos who?
Thermos be a better way.

Knock, knock.
Who's there?
Element.
Element who?
Element to tell you that she can't see
    you today.

Knock, knock.
Who's there?
Comet.
Comet who?
Comet a crime, go to jail.

Knock, knock.
Who's there?
Dummy.
Dummy who?
Will you dummy a favor, please?

Knock, knock.
Who's there?
Meter.
Meter who?
Let's meter at the park.

Knock, knock.
Who's there?
Beehive.
Beehive who?
Beehive yourself or else.

Knock, knock.
Who's there?
Lass.
Lass who?
That's what cowboys use to rope
    calves, isn't it?

Knock, knock.
Who's there?
Unit.
Unit who?
Unit me such a beautiful scarf!

Knock, knock.
Who's there?
Throat.
Throat who?
Throat out if it's spoiled.

Knock, knock.
Who's there?
Pencil.
Pencil who?
Your pencil fall down if you
    don't wear a belt.

Knock, knock.
Who's there?
Chimney.
Chimney who?
Chimney Cricket. Have you seen
Pinocchio?

Knock, knock.
Who's there?
Summertime.
Summertime who?
Summertime you can be a real pest.

Knock, knock.
Who's there?
Statue.
Statue who?
It's me. Statue?

Knock, knock.
Who's there?
Ammonia.
Ammonia who?
Ammonia going to tell you once,
    so listen carefully.

Knock, knock.
Who's there?
Cotton.
Cotton who?
I'm cotton a trap—please get me out!

Knock, knock.
Who's there?
Scissor.
Scissor who?
Scissor and Cleopatra.

Knock, knock.
Who's there?
Dishes.
Dishes who?
Dishes me. Can I come in?

Knock, knock.
Who's there?
Dozen.
Dozen who?
Dozen anyone want to let me in?

Knock, knock.
Who's there?
Tank.
Tank who?
You're welcome.

Knock, knock.
Who's there?
Omega.
Omega who?
Omega best player win.

Knock, knock.
Who's there?
Ooze.
Ooze who?
Ooze in charge here?

Knock, knock.
Who's there?
Jewel.
Jewel who?
Jewel be sorry when the principal finds out.

Knock, knock.
Who's there?
Button.
Button who?
Button is not polite.

Knock, knock.
Who's there?
Myth.
Myth who?
Myth you, too.

Knock, knock.
Who's there?
Jupiter.
Jupiter who?
Jupiter fly in my soup?

Knock, knock.
Who's there?
Heaven.
Heaven who?
Heaven seen you in ages.

Knock, knock.
Who's there?
Cash.
Cash who?
Cash me if you can.

Knock, knock.
Who's there?
Nuisance.
Nuisance who?
What's nuisance yesterday?

Knock, knock.
Who's there?
Underwear.
Underwear who?
I underwear I left my shoes.

Knock, knock.
Who's there?
Justice.
Justice who?
Justice I thought—no one home.

Knock, knock.
Who's there?
Says.
Says who?
Says me, that's who.

Knock, knock.
Who's there?
House.
House who?
Hi, house you doing?

Knock, knock.

Who's there?

Diploma.

Diploma who?

Call diploma to fix de leak.

Knock, knock.

Who's there?

Razor.

Razor who?

Razor hand if you know the answer.

Knock, knock.
Who's there?
Eyesore.
Eyesore who?
Eyesore do like you.

Knock, knock.
Who's there?
Dots.
Dots who?
Dots not important.

Knock, knock.
Who's there?
Sofa.
Sofa who?
Sofa so good.

Knock, knock.
Who's there?
Hallways.
Hallways who?
Why are you hallways late?

Knock, knock.
Who's there?
Quill.
Quill who?
Quill we meet again?

Knock, knock.
Who's there?
Window.
Window who?
Window we eat?

Knock, knock.

Who's there?

Accordion.

Accordion who?

Accordion to the weather report,
  it's going to rain tomorrow.

Knock, knock.

Who's there?

Needle.

Needle who?

Needle little help with your homework?

Knock, knock.
Who's there?
Tail.
Tail who?
Tail everyone you know.

Knock, knock.
Who's there?
Leaf.
Leaf who?
Leaf me alone.

Knock, knock.
Who's there?
Thumb.
Thumb who?
Thumb like it hot and thumb like it cold.

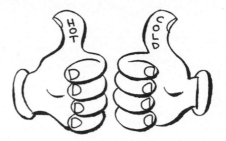

Knock, knock.
Who's there?
Hot air.
Hot air who?
Hot air, pardner, how ya doin'?

Knock, knock.
Who's there?
Wheel.
Wheel who?
Wheel stop coming over if we're not invited.

Knock, knock.
Who's there?
Despair.
Despair who?
Despair tire is flat.

Knock, knock.

Who's there?

Mission.

Mission who?

Mission you lots—wish you were here!

Knock, knock.

Who's there?

Radio.

Radio who?

Radio not, here I come.

...21, 22, 23, 24, 25!

Knock, knock.
Who's there?
One shoe.
One shoe who?
One shoe let me in?

Knock, knock.
Who's there?
Stopwatch.
Stopwatch who?
Stopwatch you're doing and open the door.

Knock, knock.
Who's there?
Tennis.
Tennis who?
Tennis five plus five.

Knock, knock.
Who's there?
Wooden shoe.
Wooden shoe who?
Wooden shoe like to know?

Knock, knock.
Who's there?
Heart.
Heart who?
It's heart to hear you—
        speak up.

Knock, knock.
Who's there?
Hair.
Hair who?
Hair today, gone tomorrow.

Knock, knock.
Who's there?
Ear.
Ear who?
Ear you are. I've been looking everywhere.

Knock, knock.
Who's there?
Canoe.
Canoe who?
Canoe come out and play with me?

Knock, knock.
Who's there?
Moustache.
Moustache who?
Wait, I moustache you a question.

Knock, knock.
Who's there?
Garden.
Garden who?
A dragon is garden the treasure.

Knock, knock.
Who's there?
Pasture.
Pasture who?
Pasture bedtime, isn't it?

Knock, knock.
Who's there?
Army.
Army who?
Army and you still friends?

Knock, knock.
Who's there?
Torch.
Torch who?
Torch you'd never ask.

Go, Girls!

The Name Game

Knock, knock.
Who's there?
Abby.
Abby who?
Abby stung me on my nose.

Knock, knock.
Who's there?
Effie.
Effie who?
Effie'd known you were coming,
he'd have baked a cake.

Knock, knock.
Who's there?
Stephanie.
Stephanie who?
It's Stephanie going to be sunny today.

Knock, knock.
Who's there?
Faith.
Faith who?
Time to Faith the music.

Knock, knock.
Who's there?
Alison.
Alison who?
Alison to you if you'll listen to me.

Knock, knock.
Who's there?
Amanda.
Amanda who?
Amanda fix the refrigerator is here.

Knock, knock.
Who's there?
Wanda.
Wanda who?
Wanda come out and play?

Knock, knock.
Who's there?
Amy.
Amy who?
Amy in the right direction.

Knock, knock.
Who's there?
Annie.
Annie who?
Annie one home?

Knock, knock.
Who's there?
Isabelle.
Isabelle who?
Isabelle on the cat's collar?

Knock, knock.
Who's there?
Lorraine.
Lorraine who?
Lorraine is falling. Where's my umbrella?

Knock, knock.
Who's there?
Aurora.
Aurora who?
Aurora's just come from that big polar bear.

Knock, knock.
Who's there?
Avery.
Avery who?
Avery time I come to see you we go
    through this.

Knock, knock.
Who's there?
Minnie.
Minnie who?
Minnie more miles to go.

Knock, knock.
Who's there?
Barbara.
Barbara who?
"Barbara black sheep, have you any
  wool . . . ?"

Knock, knock.
Who's there?
Barbie.
Barbie who?
Barbie Q.

Knock, knock.
Who's there?
Ben and Anna.
Ben and Anna who?
Ben and Anna split—they're gone.

Knock, knock.
Who's there?
Candice.
Candice who?
Candice be true?

Knock, knock.
Who's there?
Agatha.
Agatha who?
Agatha headache. Do you have an aspirin?

Knock, knock.
Who's there?
Erma.
Erma who?
"Erma a little teapot,
    short and stout . . ."

Knock, knock.
Who's there?
Carmen.
Carmen who?
Carmen get it.

Knock, knock.
Who's there?
Emma.
Emma who?
Emma bit cold out here—please let me in.

Knock, knock.
Who's there?
Daisy.
Daisy who?
Daisy wakes, nights he sleeps.

Knock, knock.
Who's there?
Denise.
Denise who?
Denise are above de ankles.

Knock, knock.
Who's there?
Diane.
Diane who?
I'm Diane to meet you.

Knock, knock.
Who's there?
Eileen.
Eileen who?
Eileen over to tie my shoes.

Knock, knock.
Who's there?
Elizabeth.
Elizabeth who?
Elizabeth of knowledge is a dangerous
   thing.

Knock, knock.
Who's there?
Gwen.
Gwen who?
Gwen fishin'.

Knock, knock.
Who's there?
Esther.
Esther who?
Esther anything I can do for you?

Knock, knock.
Who's there?
Fiona.
Fiona who?
Fiona lookout for Mom and Dad.

Knock, knock.
Who's there?
Doris.
Doris who?
The Doris locked—that's why I'm
    knocking.

Knock, knock.
Who's there?
Frances.
Frances who?
Frances in Europe.

Knock, knock.
Who's there?
Gwen.
Gwen who?
Gwen ever you wish.

Knock, knock.
Who's there?
Ginny.
Ginny who?
Ginny a hug.

Knock, knock.
Who's there?
Sacha.
Sacha who?
You make Sacha fuss!

Knock, knock.
Who's there?
Tamara.
Tamara who?
Tamara is Tuesday.

Knock, knock.
Who's there?
Maya.
Maya who?
Maya best friend?

Knock, knock.
Who's there?
Beth.
Beth who?
The Beth time ever.

Knock, knock.
Who's there?
Phyllis.
Phyllis who?
Phyllis in on all the news.

Knock, knock.
Who's there?
Thea.
Thea who?
Thea later, alligator.

Knock, knock.
Who's there?
Violet.
Violet who?
Violet that go to waste?

Knock, knock.
Who's there?
Harriet.
Harriet who?
Harriet up—we're late.

Knock, knock.
Who's there?
Ida.
Ida who?
Ida terrible time getting here.

Knock, knock.
Who's there?
Lauren.
Lauren who?
Lauren order.

Knock, knock.
Who's there?
Jess.
Jess who?
Jess me and my shadow.

Knock, knock.
Who's there?
Izzy.
Izzy who?
Izzy come, Izzy go.

Knock, knock.
Who's there?
Joan.
Joan who?
Joan call us—we'll call you.

Knock, knock.
Who's there?
Joanne.
Joanne who?
Joanne tell.

Knock, knock.
Who's there?
Adair.
Adair who?
Adair to be different.

Knock, knock.
Who's there?
Julie.
Julie who?
Why don't Julie me alone?

Knock, knock.
Who's there?
Kim.
Kim who?
I Kim too late for the movie.

Knock, knock.
Who's there?
Ida.
Ida who?
Ida know, I gotta ask.

Knock, knock.
Who's there?
Lena.
Lena who?
Lena little closer—I have something
    to tell you.

Knock, knock.
Who's there?
Meg.
Meg who?
Meg up your mind.

Knock, knock.
Who's there?
Danielle.
Danielle who?
Danielle at me—it's not my fault.

Knock, knock.
Who's there?
Maura.
Maura who?
The Maura the merrier.

Knock, knock.
Who's there?
Hannah.
Hannah who?
"Hannah partridge in a pear tree . . ."

Knock, knock.
Who's there?
Morgan.
Morgan who?
Morgan I expected.

Knock, knock.
Who's there?
Olive.
Olive who?
Olive the pizza was gone before I got a slice.

Knock, knock.
Who's there?
Nana.
Nana who?
It's Nana your business.

Knock, knock.
Who's there?
Petunia.
Petunia who?
There's a problem Petunia and me.

Knock, knock.
Who's there?
Quincy.
Quincy who?
You Quincy the doctor now.

Knock, knock.
Who's there?
Rhoda.
Rhoda who?
"Row, row, Rhoda boat gently down the
stream . . ."

Knock, knock.
Who's there?
Peg.
Peg who?
Peg your pardon—I've got the wrong door.

Knock, knock.
Who's there?
Marietta.
Marietta who?
Marietta whole cake.

Knock, knock.
Who's there?
Rita.
Rita who?
Rita book—it's fun.

Knock, knock.
Who's there?
Ruth.
Ruth who?
The Ruth of the matter is, I like you.

Knork, knork.
Who's there?
Shirley.
Shirley who?
There Shirley must be something wrong
with your door knocker.

Knock, knock.
Who's there?
Sally.
Sally who?
Sally dance?

Knock, knock.
Who's there?
Sandy.
Sandy who?
Sandy door—I just got a splinter.

Knock, knock.
Who's there?
Sarah.
Sarah who?
Sarah reason you're not laughing?

Knock, knock.
Who's there?
Sadie.
Sadie who?
I can Sadie ten times table without any
     mistakes.

Knock, knock.
Who's there?
Stacey.
Stacey who?
Stacey'ted until the bus stops.

Knock, knock.
Who's there?
Theresa.
Theresa who?
Theresa fly in my soup.

Knock, knock.
Who's there?
Sharon.
Sharon who?
Sharon share alike.

Knock, knock.
Who's there?
Sophie.
Sophie who?
Sophie me—I'm hungry.

Knock, knock.
Who's there?
Shelby.
Shelby who?
"Shelby comin' round the mountain when
she comes . . ."

Knock, knock.
Who's there?
Lana.
Lana who?
This is the Lana the free.

Knock, knock.
Who's there?
Wendy.
Wendy who?
"Wendy wind blows, de cradle will
   rock . . ."

Knock, knock.
Who's there?
Mandy.
Mandy who?
Mandy lifeboats—de ship is sinking.

Knock, knock.
Who's there?
Mara.
Mara who?
"Mara, Mara on the wall . . ."

Snow Kidding

(Way) Out in the Cold

Knock, knock.
Who's there?
Guitar.
Guitar who?
Let's guitar coats—it's cold outside.

Knock, knock.

Who's there?

Ice floe.

Ice floe who?

Ice floe-ting in the cold water—please pull me out.

Knock, knock.

Who's there?

Wet.

Wet who?

Wet me in—it's waining!

Knock, knock.
Who's there?
Snow.
Snow who?
There's snow business like
    show business.

Knock, knock.
Who's there?
Blue.
Blue who?
Blue your nose—it's running.

Knock, knock.
Who's there?
Icy.
Icy who?
Icy you opening the door!

Knock, knock.
Who's there?
Arctics.
Arctics who?
Arctics going to bite me in the woods?

Knock, knock.
Who's there?
Hatch.
Hatch who?
Ha ha—made you sneeze!

Knock, knock.
Who's there?
Sleet.
Sleet who?
Sleet—I'm starving.

Knock, knock.
Who's there?
Snowy.
Snowy who?
Snowy in the word snow—it's spelled
s-n-o-w.

Knock, knock.
Who's there?
Tis.
Tis who?
Tis who is good to wipe your nose with.

Knock, knock.
Who's there?
Snow.
Snow who?
Snow skating today—the ice is too thin.

Knock, knock.
Who's there?
Shivery.
Shivery who?
Shivery disappeared with the Knights
of the Round Table.

Knock, knock.
Who's there?
Eskimo.
Eskimo who?
Eskimo questions, I'll tell you no lies.

Knock, knock.
Who's there?
Freeze.
Freeze who?
"Freeze a jolly good fellow, freeze a
      jolly good fellow . . ."

Knock, knock.
Who's there?
Snow.
Snow who?
Snow use—I'll never finish on time.

Knock, knock.
Who's there?
Igloo.
Igloo who?
Igloo knew Susie, you'd like her.

Knock, knock.
Who's there?
Frostbite.
Frostbite who?
Frostbite your food, then chew it.

Knock, knock.
Who's there?
Scold.
Scold who?
Scold outside.

Knock, knock.
Who's there?
Icy.
Icy who?
Icy a big polar bear.

Boy Oh Boys!

What's in a Name?

Knock, knock.
Who's there?
Dwayne.
Dwayne who?
Dwayne the bathtub—I'm dwowning.

Knock, knock.
Who's there?
Arthur.
Arthur who?
Arthur any more cookies in the
cupboard?

Knock, knock.
Who's there?
Alec.
Alec who?
Alec coffee, but I don't like tea.

Knock, knock.
Who's there?
Vaughn.
Vaughn who?
Vaughn plus Vaughn equals two.

Knock, knock.
Who's there?
Barry.
Barry who?
Barry glad to see you.

Knock, knock.
Who's there?
Osborne.
Osborne who?
Osborne today. It's my birthday.

Knock, knock.
Who's there?
Dale.
Dale who?
Dale come when you call.

Knock, knock.
Who's there?
Norton.
Norton who?
I've got Norton to say.

Knock, knock.
Who's there?
Thurston.
Thurston who?
I'm Thurston for a cool drink.

Knock, knock.
Who's there?
Bjorn.
Bjorn who?
Bjorn to run.

Knock, knock.
Who's there?
Adam.
Adam who?
Adam up and tell me the total.

Knock, knock.
Who's there?
Carl.
Carl who?
A Carl get you there faster than a bike.

Knock, knock.
Who's there?
Thatcher.
Thatcher who?
Thatcher idea of a good joke?

Knock, knock.
Who's there?
Xavier.
Xavier who?
Xavier money for a rainy day.

Knock, knock.
Who's there?
Gary.
Gary who?
Gary on smiling!

Knock, knock.
Who's there?
Brad.
Brad who?
I'm afraid I have Brad news.

Knock, knock.
Who's there?
Jose.
Jose who?
"Jose, can you see . . . ?"

Knock, knock.
Who's there?
Keith.
Keith who?
Keith away from the edge!

Knock, knock.
Who's there?
Jack.
Jack who?
Jack your coats at the door.

Knock, knock.

Who's there?

Foster.

Foster who?

Foster than a speeding bullet!

Knock, knock.

Who's there?

Hurley.

Hurley who?

Hurley to bed, Hurley to rise.

Knock, knock.
Who's there?
Earl.
Earl who?
Earl be glad when vacation starts.

Knock, knock.
Who's there?
Benjamin.
Benjamin who?
Benjamin with the band all night.

Knock, knock.
Who's there?
Thaddeus.
Thaddeus who?
To be or not to be, Thaddeus the question.

Knock, knock.
Who's there?
Ahmed.
Ahmed who?
Ahmed a big mistake coming here.

Knock, knock.
Who's there?
Alex.
Alex who?
Alex plain later—just let me in.

Knock, knock.
Who's there?
Alvin.
Alvin who?
Alvin a great time, how about you?

Knock, knock.
Who's there?
Amos.
Amos who?
Amos-quito bit me.

Knock, knock.
Who's there?
Arnold.
Arnold who?
Arnold friend you haven't seen for years.

Knock, knock.
Who's there?
Hammond.
Hammond who?
I like Hammond eggs for breakfast.

Knock, knock.
Who's there?
Ben.
Ben who?
Ben knocking on this door all morning.

Knock, knock.
Who's there?
Bond.
Bond who?
You're Bond to succeed if you work hard.

Knock, knock.
Who's there?
Colin.
Colin who?
I'm Colin the doctor because I'm sick.

Knock, knock.
Who's there?
Darwin.
Darwin who?
I'll be Darwin you open de door.

Knock, knock.
Who's there?
Dewey.
Dewey who?
Dewey have to listen to all this
  knocking?

Knock, knock.
Who's there?
Dennis.
Dennis who?
Dennis is my favorite game.

Knock, knock.
Who's there?
Grover.
Grover who?
Please Grover there and get me
    a cookie.

Knock, knock.
Who's there?
Gabe.
Gabe who?
I Gabe it everything I've got.

Knock, knock.
Who's there?
Douglas.
Douglas who?
Douglas is broken—don't cut yourself.

Knock, knock.
Who's there?
Jethro.
Jethro who?
Jethro the boat and stop asking questions.

Knock, knock.
Who's there?
Eddie.
Eddie who?
Is Eddie body home?

Knock, knock.
Who's there?
Ethan.
Ethan who?
You are Ethan me out of houth
  and home.

Knock, knock.
Who's there?
Les.
Les who?
Les go for a swim.

Knock, knock.
Who's there?
Evan.
Evan who?
Evan and Earth.

Knock, knock.
Who's there?
Farley.
Farley who?
Farley the leader.

Knock, knock.
Who's there?
Dwight.
Dwight who?
There's Dwight way and there's
    de wrong way.

Knock, knock.
Who's there?
Freddie.
Freddie who?
Freddie or not, here I come.

Knock, knock.
Who's there?
Felix.
Felix who?
Felix my ice cream again, he'll be in trouble.

Knock, knock.
Who's there?
Ezra.
Ezra who?
Ezra no hope for me?

Knock, knock.
Who's there?
Lionel.
Lionel who?
Lionel bite you if you put your head in its
    mouth.

Knock, knock.
Who's there?
Bruce.
Bruce who?
I have a Bruce on my shin.

Knock, knock.
Who's there?
Buddha.
Buddha who?
Please Buddha this slice of bread for me.

Knock, knock.
Who's there?
Luke.
Luke who?
Luke through the
    keyhole and you'll see.

Knock, knock.
Who's there?
General Lee.
General Lee who?
General Lee I do not tell knock-knock jokes.

Knock, knock.
Who's there?
Gino.
Gino who?
Gino me—now open the door!

Knock, knock.
Who's there?
Gus.
Gus who?
That's what *you're* supposed to do.

Knock, knock.
Who's there?
Hank.
Hank who?
You're welcome.

Knock, knock.
Who's there?
Juan.
Juan who?
Juan of these days, you'll open the door.

Knock, knock.
Who's there?
Kenneth.
Kenneth who?
Kenneth little kids play with you?

Knock, knock.
Who's there?
Sherwood.
Sherwood who?
Sherwood like some ice cream.

Knock, knock.
Who's there?
Harold.
Harold who?
I'm eleven—Harold are you?

Knock, knock.
Who's there?
Randy.
Randy who?
I Randy mile in eight minutes.

Knock, knock.
Who's there?
Isadore.
Isadore who?
Isadore bell here? I'm tired of knocking.

Knock, knock.
Who's there?
Howard.
Howard who?
Howard I know?

Knock, knock.
Who's there?
Howie.
Howie who?
Howie going to figure this out?

Knock, knock.
Who's there?
Eisenhower.
Eisenhower who?
Eisenhower late getting here.

Knock, knock.
Who's there?
Jess.
Jess who?
I give up—who?

Knock, knock.
Who's there?
Dimitri.
Dimitri who?
Dimitri is where de hamburgers grow.

Knock, knock.
Who's there?
Justin.
Justin who?
You're Justin time.

Knock, knock.
Who's there?
Tex.
Tex who?
It Tex two to tango.

Knock, knock.
Who's there?
Kent.
Kent who?
Kent you tell by my voice?

Knock, knock.
Who's there?
Matthew.
Matthew who?
Matthew is pinthing my foot.

Knock, knock.
Who's there?
Ivan.
Ivan who?
Ivan my money back.

Knock, knock.
Who's there?
Mort.
Mort who?
Mort to the point, who are you?

Knock, knock.
Who's there?
Max.
Max who?
It Max no difference—open the door.

Knock, knock.
Who's there?
Tyrone.
Tyrone who?
Tyrone shoelaces.

Knock, knock.
Who's there?
Oscar.
Oscar who?
Oscar silly question, get a silly answer.

Knock, knock.
Who's there?
Noel.
Noel who?
Noel bows on the table, please.

Knock, knock.
Who's there?
Ivan.
Ivan who?
Ivan working on the railroad.

Knock, knock.
Who's there?
Ken.
Ken who?
Ken you open the door and let me in?

Knock, knock.
Who's there?
Mikey.
Mikey who?
Mikey won't fit in this lock.

Knock, knock.
Who's there?
Mister.
Mister who?
Mister at the bus stop—
   do you know where she is?

Knock, knock.
Who's there?
Morrison.
Morrison who?
The Morrison, the more I tan.

Knock, knock.
Who's there?
Paul.
Paul who?
Paul up a chair and I'll tell you.

Knock, knock.
Who's there?
Sam.
Sam who?
Sam person who knocked last time.

Knock, knock.
Who's there?
Mozart.
Mozart who?
Mozart is in found in museums.

Knock, knock.
Who's there?
Theodore.
Theodore who?
Theodore is shut—please open it.

Knock, knock.
Who's there?
Ozzie.
Ozzie who?
Ozzie you later, alligator.

Knock, knock.
Who's there?
Philip.
Philip who?
Philip the gas tank—I'm running low.

Knock, knock.
Who's there?
Stevie.
Stevie who?
Stevie on? Please turn it off.

Knock, knock.
Who's there?
Tarzan.
Tarzan who?
Tarzan stripes forever.

Knock, knock.
Who's there?
Oliver.
Oliver who?
Oliver troubles are over.

Knock, knock.
Who's there?
Stu.
Stu who?
Stu late now.

Knock, knock.
Who's there?
Tobias.
Tobias who?
Tobias some ice cream, you need
some money.

Knock, knock.
Who's there?
Toby.
Toby who?
Toby or not Toby, that is the question.

Knock, knock.
Who's there?
Noah.
Noah who?
Noah good place to eat?

Knock, knock.
Who's there?
Stan.
Stan who?
Stan back—you're too close.

Knock, knock.
Who's there?
Micah.
Micah who?
Hurry up—Micah is double-parked.

Knock, knock.
Who's there?
Watson.
Watson who?
Watson TV tonight?

Knock, knock.
Who's there?
Zeke.
Zeke who?
Zeke and you shall find . . .

Knock, knock.
Who's there?
Darryl.
Darryl who?
Darryl never be another you.

Knock, knock.
Who's there?
Jimmy.
Jimmy who?
Jimmy a chance, will you?

Knock, knock.
Who's there?
Scott.
Scott who?
Scott nothing to do with you.

Knock, knock.
Who's there?
Abe.
Abe who?
Abe C D E F G H . . .

Knock, knock.
Who's there?
Simon.
Simon who?
Simon the dotted line.

Around the Whirl

Where Are We Now?

Knock, knock.
Who's there?
Hawaii.
Hawaii who?
Fine, Hawaii you?

Knock, knock.
Who's there?
Italian.
Italian who?
Italian you for the last time—
    open this door!

Knock, knock.
Who's there?
Turkey.
Turkey who?
Turkey, open door.

Knock, knock.
Who's there?
Yukon.
Yukon who?
Yukon say that again.

Knock, knock.
Who's there?
Genoa.
Genoa who?
Genoa any new jokes?

Knock, knock.
Who's there?
Odessa.
Odessa who?
Odessa good one!

Knock, knock.
Who's there?
Florida.
Florida who?
The Florida bathroom is wet.

Knock, knock.
Who's there?
Madrid.
Madrid who?
Madrid you wash my jeans?

Knock, knock.
Who's there?
Sicily.
Sicily who?
That's a Sicily question.

Knock, knock.
Who's there?
Tennessee.
Tennessee who?
Tennessee you later?

Knock, knock.
Who's there?
Cuba.
Cuba who?
Cuba ice.

Knock, knock.
Who's there?
Alaska.
Alaska who?
Alaska you another if you don't like-a this one.

Knock, knock.
Who's there?
Venice.
Venice who?
Venice this door going to open?

Knock, knock.
Who's there?
Valencia.
Valencia who?
Valencia dollar, will you pay it back?

Knock, knock.
Who's there?
Sultan.
Sultan who?
Sultan pepper.

Knock, knock.
Who's there?
Uganda.
Uganda who?
Uganda get away with this!

Knock, knock.
Who's there?
Kentucky.
Kentucky who?
Dad Kentucky you in at night.

Knock, knock.
Who's there?
Burma.
Burma who?
I Burma hand on the stove.

Knock, knock.
Who's there?
Jamaica.
Jamaica who?
Jamaica good grade on your math test?

Knock, knock.
Who's there?
Atlas.
Atlas who?
Atlas, it's the weekend!

Knock, knock.
Who's there?
Nantucket.
Nantucket who?
Nantucket, but she'll give it back.

Knock, knock.
Who's there?
Utah.
Utah who?
Utah a puddy tat?

Knock, knock.
Who's there?
Norway.
Norway who?
Norway will I leave till you open this door.

Knock, knock.
Who's there?
Minsk.
Minsk who?
Minsk-meat pie.

Knock, knock.
Who's there?
Mecca.
Mecca who?
You Mecca me happy.

Knock, knock.
Who's there?
Safari.
Safari who?
Safari so good . . .

Knock, knock.
Who's there?
Japan.
Japan who?
Ouch, Japan is too hot.

Knock, knock.
Who's there?
Kenya.
Kenya who?
Kenya guess who it is?

Knock, knock.
Who's there?
Hacienda.
Hacienda who?
Hacienda the story.

Knock, knock.
Who's there?
Sweden.
Sweden who?
Sweden sour chicken is my favorite.

Knock, knock.
Who's there?
Perth.
Perth who?
A Perth full of cointh.

Knock, knock.
Who's there?
Spain.
Spain who?
Spain to have to keep knocking on this door!

Knock, knock.
Who's there?
Isle.
Isle who?
Isle ask the questions around here.

Knock, knock.
Who's there?
Utah King.
Utah King who?
Utah King to me?

Knock, knock.
Who's there?
Irish.
Irish who?
Irish you would let me in.

Knock, knock.
Who's there?
Oslo.
Oslo who?
Oslo down—there's no hurry.

Knock, knock.

Who's there?

Arizona.

Arizona who?

Arizona room for one of us in this town.

Knock, knock.

Who's there?

Sheik.

Sheik who?

Sheik the carton
before you pour.

Knock, knock.
Who's there?
Armenia.
Armenia who?
Armenia every word I say.

Knock, knock.
Who's there?
Bolivia.
Bolivia who?
Bolivia me—I know what I'm talking about.

Knock, knock.
Who's there?
Cologne.
Cologne who?
Cologne me names won't help.

Knock, knock.
Who's there?
Wyoming.
Wyoming who?
Wyoming so mean to me?

Knock, knock.
Who's there?
Congo.
Congo who?
I Congo out—I'm grounded.

Knock, knock.
Who's there?
Moscow.
Moscow who?
I Moscow home soon.

Knock, knock.
Who's there?
India.
India who?
India nighttime I go to sleep.

Knock, knock.
Who's there?
Iowa.
Iowa who?
Iowa you a dollar.

Knock, knock.
Who's there?
Paris.
Paris who?
A Paris good, but I'd rather have an orange.

Knock, knock.
Who's there?
Quebec.
Quebec who?
Quebec to the end of the line.

Knock, knock.
Who's there?
Idaho.
Idaho who?
If Idaho, Idaho the whole garden.

Knock, knock.
Who's there?
Germany.
Germany who?
Germany people are knocking at
    your door?

Knock, knock.
Who's there?
Minneapolis.
Minneapolis who?
Minneapolis a day keeps many doctors away.

Knock, knock.
Who's there?
Missouri.
Missouri who?
Missouri loves company.

Knock, knock.
Who's there?
Uruguay.
Uruguay who?
You go Uruguay and I'll go mine.

Knock, knock.
Who's there?
Europe.
Europe who?
I can tell Europe to no good.

Knock, knock.
Who's there?
Egypt.
Egypt who?
Egypt you when he sold you a broken doorbell.

Knock, knock.
Who's there?
Alaska.
Alaska who?
Alaska my mom if I can come out
and play.

Knock, knock.
Who's there?
Tibet.
Tibet who?
Early Tibet and early to rise.

Knock, knock.
Who's there?
Texas.
Texas who?
Texas are getting higher every year.

Knock, knock.
Who's there?
Indonesia.
Indonesia who?
Spiders make me weak ⟨ Indonesia.

Knock, knock.
Who's there?
Juneau.
Juneau who?
Juneau where Alaska is?

Knock, knock.
Who's there?
Iran.
Iran who?
Iran hard to get here.

Knock, knock.
Who's there?
Berlin.
Berlin who?
I'm Berlin the water for hard-boiled eggs.

Knock, knock.
Who's there?
Ghana.
Ghana who?
We're Ghana go to the movies.

Knock, knock.
Who's there?
Sahara.
Sahara who?
Sahara you feeling today?

Knock, knock.
Who's there?
Galway.
Galway who?
Galway and leave me alone.

Knock, knock.
Who's there?
Israeli.
Israeli who?
Israeli good to be here.

Knock, knock.
Who's there?
Samoa.
Samoa who?
Yes, please, I'd like Samoa.

Knock, knock.
Who's there?
Aspen.
Aspen who?
When Aspen around I get dizzy.

Knock, knock.
Who's there?
Dublin.
Dublin who?
The cost of milk is Dublin.

Knock, knock.
Who's there?
Fresno.
Fresno who?
Fresno fun when he's grouchy.

Knock, knock.
Who's there?
Havana.
Havana who?
We're Havana great time.

Say That Again?

Words to Play On

Knock, knock.
Who's there?
Zone.
Zone who?
He's scared of his zone shadow.

Knock, knock.
Who's there?
Argue.
Argue who?
Argue going to let me in or not?

Knock, knock.
Who's there?
Sparkle.
Sparkle who?
A sparkle start a fire if you're not careful.

Knock, knock.
Who's there?
Passion.
Passion who?
I was just passion through and thought
I'd say hello.

Knock, knock.
Who's there?
Juicy.
Juicy who?
Juicy what I saw?

Knock, knock.
Who's there?
Cozy.
Cozy who?
Cozy who's knocking.

Knock, knock.
Who's there?
Waddle.
Waddle who?
Waddle you give me if I go away?

Knock, knock.
Who's there?
Dimension.
Dimension who?
That's OK, dimension it.

Knock, knock.
Who's there?
Typhoid.
Typhoid who?
Typhoid that song before.

Knock, knock.
Who's there?
Zoom.
Zoom who?
Zoom did you expect?

Knock, knock.
Who's there?
Miniature.
Miniature who?
The miniature open the door I'll tell you.

Knock, knock.
Who's there?
Noise.
Noise who?
It's noise to see you.

Knock, knock.

Who's there?

I-8.

I-8 who?

Thanks, but I-8 lunch already.

Knock, knock.

Who's there?

Wah.

Wah who?

Well, you don't have to
get so excited about it.

Knock, knock.
Who's there?
Sincerely.
Sincerely who?
I've been waiting sincerely this morning.

Knock, knock.
Who's there?
Repeat.
Repeat who?
Who, who, who . . .

Knock, knock.
Who's there?
Toothy.
Toothy who?
Toothy is the day after Monday.

Knock, knock.
Who's there?
Value.
Value who?
Value be my Valentine?

Knock, knock.
Who's there?
Dime.
Dime who?
Dime to go to bed.

Knock, knock.
Who's there?
Zany.
Zany who?
Zany body home?

Knock, knock.
Who's there?
U-C-I.
U-C-I who?
U-C-I had to ring because you didn't
   answer when I knocked.

Knock, knock.
Who's there?
Sonata.
Sonata who?
Don't worry, sonata a big deal.

Knock, knock.
Who's there?
Sizzle.
Sizzle who?
Sizzle need your full attention.

Knock, knock.

Who's there?

Senior.

Senior who?

Senior being so nosy, I'm not going to tell you.

Knock, knock.

Who's there?

Thistle.

Thistle who?

Thistle be the last joke in this book.